Marriage Counseling 101:

A Practical Guide for Ministers

Patsy Highland Ph.D

Marriage Counseling 101: A Practical Guide For Ministers Copyright ©
Patsy Highland

Newburgh Press, Newburgh, Indiana
www.newburghseminary.com

Requests for Information should be addressed to Dr. Patsy Highland,
Master Resources, Inc., Suite 203, 151 Heritage Park Dr., Murfreesboro,
Tn. 37129 Phone 615-895-0787, www.mripjh@aol.com; Website www.
masterresources.com ;

ISBN: 978-0-9790625-1-3

Printed in the United States of America

Contents

Note to Reader

This book began as a required step in earning my Ph.D. in counseling. Through the encouragement of several allies and friends in the process, I realized this may be a helpful guide to pastors and other ministry related persons who desire to help build strong marriages.

A book like this is more than an academic project. It is a large part of my life and learning, condensed and organized into words. From my childhood, the churches and the ministers who served them have been very important and have helped shape my writing. Living in the roles of pastor's wife, public school teacher, Bible teacher and conference leader, being an adult student, counselor and director of a staff of counselors has prepared me to offer the message of this book.

In the journey of becoming a member of this helping profession and writing this book about the ministry of counseling, I owe an enormous debt to so many. To the authors of the books used as resources, the professors who taught me, the supervisors and conference leaders in my continuing education, and to my colleagues in counseling, I say thank you. I am especially indebted to Jean Cotey, one of my favorite pastor wives, a gifted writer and teacher, who tirelessly edited my work. To Linda Williams and Tanya Gilmore, my administrative assistants who typed and retyped the manuscript, thank you so much.

Most of all I honor and thank the most important member of my team, my beloved husband, Jim Highland. He brought to me great encouragement, help in writing the manuscript, motivation when I wanted to quit, and most important, helped me believe in myself.

I dedicate this book to my Godly mother, Lessie Jackson, who insisted that the book be published, and provided the funds to make it happen.

Thank you for securing and opening this book. My prayer is that it will enrich your life and your ministry to those you counsel.

Patsy Highland, Ph.D.
Licensed Professional Counselor
Mental Health Service Provider

Introduction

**"Christian counseling must be dedicated to life
in the body of Christ. If Christ draws all people to
Himself when He is lifted up (John 12:32),
let us deliberately and passionately lift up Christ
in our counseling practice."
(Timothy Clinton and George Ohlschager)**

Jesus lived with an intense focus on his mission and purpose. He moved through His ministry conscious of what he called "my time," a timeline that led to the cross. He prepared His band of struggling disciples to launch His vision for the redemption of mankind. He was a man on a mission.

Nevertheless, the gospels are about more than that – his response to current human need. The gospels tell what happened in the off moments, in a journey to another city, moments when He had planned to rest and pray. These are the stories of how he responded to the appeals and needs of the common people who could not help Him in His personal mission.

For example, His first miracle at the wedding in Cana was in response to His mother's appeal for help for the host family. The lame came to ask for the privilege of walking again, the blind asked to receive

3

their sight and the diseased asked that their bodies be healed. Jesus responded to all of these as a significant way to witness about His mission and purpose.

We who wear the mantle of Jesus, who acknowledge that we represent Jesus, are also on a mission. Our mission is to help others find Jesus as Savior and guide them to grow in their relationship of claiming Him Lord. We serve on a battlefield where enemy forces want to counter our efforts and make us ineffective. In our current day there are many such confrontations with the forces of evil, and they each impact us in some way.

In this book we address the battle for healthy Christian marriages. The failure of one marriage produces failures throughout the family, with the young people coming from those homes and in the marriages formed by those children. We are unable to estimate the damage done when marriages fail. This is not just happening in the world around us. It is happening in the ranks of ministers, within the families of our congregation and among our own children.

We can choose to avoid this crisis, by hiding in our secluded world of stained glass and stately music. Scott Peck in his classic book *The*

Road Less Traveled, stated, avoidance is the beginning of mental illness.[1] He was right. This will drive us crazy! Instead, we can choose to join others on the battlefield. Bo Prosser and Charles Qualls have advised us, "Let's try to frame the discussion around healthy marriages. A healthy marriage is better than a normal marriage."[2] We will have many allies when we do. These are dedicated physicians, psychiatrists, professional therapist, social workers, school counselors and an army of others who have a role in this battle.

There are several battle stations we can fill. We can provide training opportunities for those getting married and for the married, coach those trying to do better, and provide first aid for those wounded in this battle. We in the helping professions must also see ourselves as MASH units, picking up the wounded from the battlefield and giving them a chance for healing. This book is designed to inform ministers who want to enter the battlefield as a soldier.

1.   Some who read this may choose to enter the counseling ministry with a sense of calling for long-term service.

---

[1] M. Scott Peck, *The Road Less Traveled,* (New York: Touchstone), 1978, 40.

[2] Bo Prosser and Charles Qualls, *Marriage Ministry,* (Macon: Smith and Helwys Publishing, 2004), 72.

2.   Some who read this may learn enough to give first aid and remember the physician's code of "Heal when you can, do no harm when you cannot."

3.   All who come to these pages will be helped in some way to join the battle.

Several stations we can fill:

Guarding those married and getting married,

Coaching for those doing battle,

Giving first aid for those getting wounded

While we in the helping vocation of professional counselors see ourselves as the MASH unit, picking up the wounded from behind the front line and giving them first aid and care, we need help. Our best allies are ministers. Some of them are on the battlefields, while many are cloistered in their cathedrals unaware of the battle scene.

We intend for this book to be a practical guide for ministers in marriage counseling, presented in everyday language. You will indicate to us to what degree we were successful by your response to the call to help build healthy Christian marriages.

Chapter 1

The Minister's Personal Preparation

**"The Spirit of the Lord is upon me, because the Lord
has appointed me to bring good news to the poor. He
has sent me to comfort the broken hearted and to
announce that captives will be released and prisoners
will be freed." (Isaiah 61:1)**

The Bible helps build and maintain the proper attitudes and actions

to be a Christian counselor. The presence of love and compassion and the

actions of acceptance and empathy are essential. The use of the right

words and phrases are important for the Christian counselor. These are

best found in the pages of the Bible. The confidence to speak the truth and

the courage to confront with love are learned from the scriptures.

The Christian Model, Jesus

People come to the minister for counseling primarily because of

his connection with Jesus Christ. The person of Jesus Christ, His helpful

words and His modeled life make Him the ideal model for counselors.

The Christian counselor can learn good counseling attitudes and skills by

studying the life and teachings of Jesus. In my years of preparation for

counseling many of my professors stressed the importance of doing

counseling out of whom you are. Jesus did ministry out of who He was.

When a client prepares to share his/her story with me, he/she will ask, "Will you judge me when I tell you my story?" I assure them I will not, thinking of Jesus' compassion and acceptance of me. Often I remember that I am to be a "light of hope" to clients as I assure them that they will be better as we move through the process. Jesus is our light of hope, and we desire to be a reflection of Him as we become the Christian counselor to others. Norman Wright, in his helpful book *Marriage Counseling*, states, "As we look at the characteristics of Jesus' approach to counseling, we must remember that techniques alone are not effective. Jesus' relationship with the person to whom He was ministering was the foundation of His approach."[3]

Jesus modeled the right tools as He related to others. His ability to show discernment was evident. His sense of authority in His instruction was commanding. He practiced good behavior before he asked others to perform good behavior. His title was "Rabbi" or "Teacher," because He instructed people in the art of abundant living. His boldness to practice confrontation when necessary underscored His ability to do the right thing in the right way.

---

[3] Norman H. Wright, *Marriage Counseling* (Ventura: Regal Books, 1995), 31.

Jesus modeled the right attitudes as he met with people. He was always compassionate, living a life filled with love. He practiced acceptance of any and all persons, not just those who behaved well or dressed nicely. His attitudes were marked by hope, and His words were always encouraging.

Jesus was and is a model in relationship building. That does not mean that everyone liked Him. In fact, Jesus knew better than to desire that all people like Him. All people, however, respected Him. Those who followed Him did so in love and confidence. He called His disciples "friend". Norman Wright says: "Reviewing Jesus' dealings with people, there appears an interesting relationship between the role Jesus chose to play and his style of relating. For example, when Jesus took the role of 'prophet,' he preached, taught, confronted and called for repentance. When he took the role of the 'priest' he listened, forgave, mediated and called for confession. When he assumed the role of king he paraded, ruled, and called for the establishment of the kingdom. When he chose the role of 'lamb' he sacrificed, accepted ridicule and rejection and called sinners to be healed by his stripes. When he submitted to the role of servant, he washed feet, served food, gave of himself and called for humility. When he played the role of "shepherd' he fed the flock, nurtured, protected and called for the lost to be found. If we attempt to model our counseling or relating after Jesus' example, then we like Jesus will play a variety of interventive roles as we relate redemptively to hurting people."[4]

Here are some specific ways that Jesus provides us our best model in counseling.

1. His belief in the value of each and every person,

2. His belief in the possibility of change for each person,

3. His belief in the power of God to help people change,

4. His understanding of the power of choice,

5. His convictions in the inevitable fruit of choice, sowing and reaping,

6. His confidence in the influence of another person in bringing about change,

7. His use of questions, not easy answers, in counseling people

8. His effective listening skills,

9. His practice of prayer,

10. His life of faith and obedience to God,

---

[4] Norman H. Wright, *Marriage Counseling* (Ventura: Regal Books, 1995), 318-319.

What We Can Learn From the Bible

The Bible is a primary textbook for Christian Counselors. As a minister, a committed student of the Bible, you will search the Bible for help in counseling. As a committed student, you will understand it is not a detailed guidebook on counseling, but a resource book. However, you also know that the basic principles found in the Bible become the foundation for Christian counseling.

As a minister, one must be very careful that current culture does not interpret scripture but that scripture interprets current culture. The current Christian community of the minister will have specific issues that are highlighted at that time and in that culture. As a student of the Bible, the counseling minister must be aware of those issues and develop a balanced view of each issue in light of the total Biblical message.

Often the counseling ministry of the minister is seen as advice giving or simply solutions to smooth things over. Counseling is basically an enabling process for healing and growth. That process takes time, patience, wisdom and motivation in order to create meaningful change. A helpful verse of scripture is Romans 12:1-3, "be transformed by the renewing of your mind, that you may prove what is that good and acceptable and perfect will of God." We have found that there are some

11

basic principles of the Bible that shape the attitudes and content of Christian counseling. Here are some that are the foundation to our counseling practice.

(1)   The Bible demonstrates the effect that God's power has in the lives of people. The Bible is primarily a book of stories about people's lives. There are stories of victories and defeats, champions and losers. The key difference in these persons is their willingness to allow God's power to shape their lives or their refusal to do so.

(2)   The Bible demonstrates the ability of people to change, both in positive and in negative ways. There are countless persons in the Scriptures who found the will and the resources to make dramatic changes. There are many other persons who could have enjoyed positive changes, but who chose to act in negative ways that led to personal failures.

(3)   The Bible shows the major impact people have on each other, positively or negatively. The first Christians in the Book of Acts grew stronger both in numbers and in individual growth through being together. They met together often, shared what possessions they had with each other and grew both bold and more loving. The minister brings to the counseling process the resources of his or her

12

personal self plus the ability to bring other people together for purposeful relationships.

(4)   The Bible shows the impact of teachers, preachers, counselors and mentors in the development of mature Christian persons. A major theme in the stories and instructions of the Bible is the power of purposeful leadership in relationships. To be a Christian is to agree to relate to Jesus Christ, see Him as our leader and mentor and to look to Him for direction. The relationships available to people in today's congregations are many. The people whom they relate with are so helpful, and the desire of every minister is to link people together in meaningful, helpful relationships that help individuals grow.

(5)   The Bible demonstrates the effectiveness of a process of personal growth as opposed to a one time, one event type of change. Jesus' invitation to his disciples was "Come. Follow me,". "I will make you …" (Matthew 4:18-20). The Apostle Paul spoke of Christian growth as moving from"milk" to "meat" diet. Christian discipleship is always a process, not a one-time fix. Counseling is a process of healing and growth, not a correct answer that will "fix the problem."

(6) The Bible demonstrates the force of both good and evil in the lives of people and champions the way of good or godliness. Counseling is a process of helping people sort out the evil in their lives and behaviors, identify the good that needs to be incorporated into their lives, and assist in the transformation of their lives.

(7) The Bible becomes a part of the counseling process as the message of the scriptures is used as a resource for change. The Bible is both a storybook of real people living real lives of faith and instructions written to real people, real groups of Christians, about how to cope with life as a Christian.

(8) The Bible shows how the Holy Spirit, the Divine Counselor, assists the minister-counselor and those in counseling in the transformation process. In every counseling session of a Christian counselor there is always a second counselor present. The Holy Spirit is active both in guiding the counselor and in instructing the counselee during each session.

A young woman came to my office one evening, appearing to be reluctant, nervous and filled with despair. After discussing the formalities of business, I ask her for what reason she came to see me. She briefly described her past experience of seeing several counselors, and her

14

understanding that we were a Christian counseling center. Then boldly and without hesitation she said, "Can you help me find God?" As simply as I knew how and using the Bible, I explained how she could find God by receiving Jesus as her Savior and begin a life of following Him. In the several sessions that followed, we built on that theme. She began to adopt meaningful life patterns into her life and to express in her life her decision to follow Jesus Christ. While I often have opportunities to show people how to become Christians, that was the most straightforward invitation I have had to do so.

Developing a Theology of Counseling

A theology of counseling is, simply put, a Biblical belief system of helping. The Christian counselor needs a theology, or belief system, that supports this area of ministry. Here are some statements from two leading Christian Counselors concerning their personal perspectives.

"Christian counseling is a way to proclaim Christ and grow His followers. Christian counseling is a gift to the church and to the world that facilitates the kind of care that Jesus promises. Christian counseling proclaims Christ to searching hearts and, by dedicated counselor/ministers, raises up people to live fully in His image."[5]

"The Christian counselor is a deeply committed servant of Jesus Christ who applies his or her God-given abilities, skills, training, knowledge and insight to the task of helping others move to personal wholeness in Christ, interpersonal competence, mental stability and spiritual maturity."[6]

Our theology for counseling finds its deepest roots in a clear understanding of God. May we presuppose that you the reader believe in the existence of God and affirm the traditional characteristics we ascribe to God? God is self-revealing. He chooses to reveal himself to us and to others because that is His nature. The life, death, burial and resurrection of Jesus demonstrate God's ultimate revelation of His love. As Christian counselors we have a unique opportunity to represent Him to the persons who meet with us.

Our theology for counseling must include a realistic view of people. This includes accepting both a person's value and a person's

---

[5] Timothy Clinton and George Ohlschlager, *Competent Christian Counseling* (Colorado Springs: Waterbrook Press, 2002), 14.

[6] G.R. Collins, *The Biblical Basis of Counseling for People Helpers* (Colorado Springs: NavPress, 1993), 21.

sinfulness. A realistic understanding of the power and destructiveness of sin is essential. It is also essential that we understand the value God places on each person and become His agent of change for people. A theology about people must include a strong commitment to the grace and hope that God has for each person.

Our theology for counseling will find its greatest strength in our faith and understanding of Jesus Christ. "The impact of what Jesus Christ does for the believing sinner results in the creation of a new person empowered to taste of the new life in a new and healthful manner."[7] This message of hope is our core belief as anxious, troubled and fallen people come to our offices for counseling

Our theology for counseling will include a prominent place for the Holy Spirit. We who have a calling to be a "soul care worker"[8] for God find confidence in these words of Jesus, "I will pray the Father, and He will give you another Helper, that He may abide with you forever... you know Him, for He dwells with you and will be in you." (John 14:16,17). The Holy Spirit produces spiritual and behavioral changes in people. Often we are the mid-wives for these birth experiences.

---

[7] Timothy Clinton and George Ohlaschlager, *Competent Christian Counseling* (Colorado Springs: WaterBrook Press, 2002), 110.

[8] David G. Benner, *Care of Souls* (Grand Rapids: Baker Books, 2000), 23.

Our theology for counseling will incorporate the Bible as the sourcebook of revelation and relationships. Even though many Christians and churches engage in what has been called "The battle of the Bible," the Bible is the book familiar and honored by most people. While clients may have had negative experiences with both the Bible and the church, it is still both a sourcebook and a guidebook for those of us representing God. While many may use the Bible to manipulate people or criticize the Bible because of their misunderstandings, it is still a very valuable textbook for life reconstruction work. More importantly, it is the book that is both "God-breathed" and "God-empowered."

Our theology for counseling should have in it firm beliefs about the place of the church in the work of God. This does not mean that Christian counseling is done only in the four walls of a church building. It does recognize that, for Christians, the church is the family of God to which we belong. Just like our physical families, the church as a family often fails to meet our ideal standards. Nevertheless, it is our best place to go for spiritual family.

The church at its best will fulfill three supporting roles to our work as Christian Counselors. It will be the spiritual hospital for the wounded, the spiritual school for continued learning and an accepting family fellowship where we and our clients find acceptance.

Finally, our theology for counseling should be a theology for living a transforming faith as it applies to real life issues. We are not advocating a rigid, sterile system of propositions to be learned and debated. Rather, it is a platform of beliefs and faith experiences that is the central core of the counseling minister. It is to be, as we suggested earlier, a theology of helping. It is the foundational principle upon which our lives are based as mentors and what drives our counseling, teaching, advising, and coaching roles.

Understanding the Minister's Role

The minister, by virtue of his role, finds himself embedded in the ongoing process of making, maintaining and repairing marriage relationships. Specifically, as a minister serving a specific congregation, the minister is usually living in his own marriage while assisting others who are doing the same thing.

Most marriage counseling is done by the minister in informal, non-structured settings. This happens both in the everyday conversations with church members and in the teaching or preaching opportunities of ministry. In such occasions it is important that the minister realize there is

19

no such thing as a casual remark about marriage. To someone listening, the remark is either an instructive or destructive word. This is decided by the positions and thought patterns of the listener. Whether the minister chooses to engage in formal marriage counseling or not, marriage counseling is an ongoing process in any congregation. Therefore, it is important that a minister sort out his beliefs and attitudes on how to handle this role.

Understand Yourself

The minister is influenced by the same factors as the parishioner. The culture, family, marriage background and experiences of the minister are always involved in the counsel given. The religious beliefs and attitudes accumulated from the past are involved. The childhood and adult experiences of the minister, particularly related to issues of intimacy and relationships, will shape his words of counsel. Personal attitudes and convictions become visible in a counseling occasion, either formally or informally. The counseling minister must have a clear understanding of himself, his beliefs and attitude, his calling and convictions.

Understand Your Role and Priorities

"In any relationship a person's behavior quickly falls into patterns, called roles. Roles help people know how to act with each other, but roles are hard to break out of when people interact in a new context, such as counseling."[9] Different from any other professional person, ministers find themselves in multiple conflicting roles. A minister may be the minister, preacher, counselor and personal friend to a member of the congregation and they may be a decision-maker on the minister's employment. A minister must carefully define the role that is to be assumed and the primary priorities that must be established. In a study of how training in marriage counseling has impact on the performance of the minister, four summation statements were made:

1. The minister must learn about himself,

2. The minister must relate to the client not up or down to them, but on the same level.

3. The minister will reassess his moral judgments.

4. Human beings in their humanity are not so bad after all.[10]

Understanding Marriage

Marriage is the union of two unique individuals who bring different backgrounds of culture, family life, economics and religious practices that

---

[9] Everett L. Worthington, Jr. and Douglas McMurry, *Marriage Conflicts* (Grand Rapids: Baker Books, 1997), 50-51.

[10] Hilda Goodwin, "Marriage Counseling and the Minister," *Journal of Religion and Health*, Vol. 3, Issue 2, (January 1964): 178.

become woven together. On the other hand, it is a relationship designed to meet the physical and emotional needs of each person, to care for children born to the union and to make worthwhile contributions to the larger community of people. These are huge expectations for two individuals to bring to one single relationship. One writer summarizes a second challenge: "Divorce and increased cohabitation are two evidences of a society that has grown afraid of committing to the ideal."[11] This brings even a greater task for the minister counselor to guide the process in moving forward. Toss in the treacherous journey that lies ahead for a marriage relationship, and many couples find themselves staring at midlife with few resources. Pressures from family, vocational, emotional and social outlets weigh heavily on a marriage. Understanding marriage is always an incomplete task.

Understanding the power of Expectations

Marriage also is challenged by the expectations that each partner brings to the union. A large part of these expectations is primarily selfish, that is, for the good of the individual partner. Another part of these expectations is that of families, friends and larger community. A final set

---

[11] Bo Prosser and Charles Qualls, *Marriage Ministry* (Macon: Smith and Helwys Publishing, 2004), 73.

of expectations is shaped by religious life. These are expectations of developing shared religious practices, participating in a religious community, and these are framed with the expectation that this union will last for the lifetime of the individual marriage partners. It is in the mixing of such grand expectations with the weaknesses of inexperienced participants that brings forth the need of marriage counseling. There is no perfect marriage and no perfect implementation plan for marriage. In *TheWarrior, The Woman, and The Christ* G.A. Studdert-Kennedy describes marriage as a 'joyous conflict', where self-conscious persons rejoice in one another's individualities and through the clash of mind on mind and will on will, work out an ever-increasing but never fully completed unity."[12] It is a lifelong process of making continual adjustments to both maintain and enrich the marriage relationship.

In his book, *Marriage Counseling,* H. Norman Wright states that married couples need to understand the following:

1.   Marriage is a gift.

2.   Marriage is an opportunity for love to be learned.

---

[12] Ginny Bridges Ireland, "I Know Who She Is," *Christian Reflections, Center for Christian Ethics, Baylor University* (April, 2006): 71.

3.   Marriage is a journey in which we as the travelers are faced with many choices and are responsible for those choices.

4.   Marriage is more affected by our inner communication than our outer communication.

5.   Marriage is more often influenced by unresolved issues from our past than we realize.

6.   Marriage is a call to servanthood.

7.   Marriage is a call to friendship.

8.   Marriage is a call to suffering.

9.   Marriage is a refining process, being refined by God into the person He wants us to be.

10.   Marriage is not an event but a way of life.

11.   Marriage involves intimacy in all areas for it to be fulfilled.

This illustrates the enormous expectations that surround a single marriage.[13]

---

[13] Norman H. Wright, *Marriage Counseling* (Ventura: Regal Books, 1995), 12-13.

Chapter 2

Qualities of Effective Christian Counselors

**"Spiritual directors (counselors) themselves participate in
a dimension of childlikeness; they sit with the person,
listening and responding to the movements of truth that
come from beyond their management and possession."
(Eugene H. Peterson)**

As a minister, you are highly motivated to be an effective

counselor. You have often read Colossians 3:23-24. "Whatever you do,

work at it with all your heart, as working for the Lord, not for men, since

you know that you will receive an inheritance from the Lord as a reward.

It is the Lord you are serving." To fulfill this scripture and your desire to

be effective as a counselor, here are some key characteristics you will

need to develop and magnify in your life. These qualities, attributes and

skills will serve you well as an effective minister-counselor.

Compassion

There is a brief statement in the short book of Jude that has been

translated, "And some have compassion, making a difference; (Jude 1:22).

The word simply means "with passion" but we have defined it as

passionate love or active empathy. This is a strong motivating force in the

life of a minister.

25

Compassion gives a strong motivation to the knowledge and skills of a counselor. We are urged in Colossians 3:12 to "...clothe yourselves with compassion..." A working definition of compassion is a feeling for another's sorrow or hardship that leads to extending help. When we exercise compassion in our work we will exert a positive force into the counseling experience that brings positive energy and results.

Trustworthiness

The effective counseling minister understands that he or she is accountable to their marriage relationship, the counseling relationship, the church served and to God. To win the full trust of our clients, we must give our very best self to the process. To be blessed in the counseling ministry, we must value even more our duty to please God. "One constant challenge is our ability to practice self-control. Self-control reconstitutes the person so that the person can truly live above the strife of the world of controlling influences. It is the spiritual freedom of Christian liberty." "If you want control of an uncontrollable situation, find self control by letting God have control of you."[14]

---

[14] John Pugh, "Improving Relationships through Spiritual Formation," *Marriage and Family: A Christian Journal*, Vol. 6, Issue 1, (2003): 79-86.

We win the trust of our clients in both small and large ways. We keep our word at all times. We fulfill all promises made. From the way we promptly meet our appointments to the huge matter of keeping confidences, we display trustworthiness. Our ethical and moral behavior demonstrates our ability to be trusted.

Confidence

Many parts of the counseling experience are contagious and confidence is one of them. The client brings to the counseling relationship the anxiety, fear and doomsday thinking of a bad set of circumstances. The counselor brings to the counseling relationship the experience of seeing similar circumstances that have been helped, the positive view of the negative setting and the skills to help a person manage his/her way through the problem. These factors build confidence in the client. The minister-counselor also offers to the counseling relationship the dual resources of a minister and a counselor.

All of these are powerful tools in counseling, but they must be guarded carefully. People judge the counselor's larger picture of effectiveness by the smaller signals they receive in the counseling process. The power of our faithfulness in scheduling, remembering, fulfilling promises and common courtesies shape their view of the ability of the counselor to lead them through the larger issues.

Self-Esteem

While this may be a popular characteristic for everyone to desire, the counseling minister must have a balanced awareness of his/her own value and personhood. Such a central characteristic in our lives gives us a personal stability that brings strength to the counseling relationship.

It is not always easy or possible to hold our own world together while we attend the needs of others. Our personal faith and relationship with God is a storehouse of resources for moments like that. H. J. Clineball has summed up this challenge with these words. "The challenge that confronts each of us is to help release this potential by becoming incarnated counselors; persons whose imperfect relationships somehow enable the liberating word to become flesh and dwell in and among us with healing power."[15]

Communication

A main theme in the training of ministers is to learn communication, verbal and non-verbal. Counselors must become very

---

[15] H.J. Clineball, *Basic Types of Pastoral Care and Counseling Resources for the Ministry of Healing and Growth*. Abingdon, Nashville, 1984.

skilled in reading the non-verbal messages of clients. Clients also are very focused on the counselor's communication – both in words and actions.

Counselors learn communication habits that we seldom evaluate. We use words and expressions often, not thinking about how it will be translated. We have body language that speaks about our thoughtfulness, focus, energy level and moods. Like the child in the home of parents, the client learns these very quickly and reacts to them. "A steady stream of positives from the minister will usually be perceived as insensitivity to the couple's pain. Rather than strengthen faith, a Pollyanna focus will weaken faith."[16]

Words are very important but words can have double meanings, different personal meaning to the client, or carry a huge load of baggage. Communication is not just about what we say, but what the client hears. Therefore, the counselor must proceed cautiously with clients, especially new clients, as the dialog progresses. You may ask the client to tell what they just heard, or to rephrase an important statement in two or three

---

[16] Everett L. Worthington, Jr. and Douglas McMurry, *Marriage Conflicts* (Grand Rapids: Baker Books, 1997), 87.

different ways. Counselors are to be artists and surgeons, using our tools of communication to bring beauty and health to others.

Flexibility

We know the old axiom, "The only constant factor in our lives is change." That applies to counseling. In fact, change is the key factor in helping clients. There are daily changes that must be taken as routine. Changes in schedules, people's attitudes, circumstances around them and us are as routine as changes in the weather. There are changes in understanding of a client or in the client's life that cause us to change our approach with the client. Change should be welcomed, often celebrated, as a sign that the Creator God is still at work. The longer we live, the more we need to be flexible and the less likely we are to embrace flexibility.

Self-Care

Burnout is a frequent reason people give for career changes or crashes. This comes from excessive work, isolation or worry. The fatigue level of the counselor is excessively high at the end of each day. Often they feel like the Old Testament scapegoat, which was burdened down with the sins of a nation and turned loose to wander in a wilderness. This may describe how you view your life as a minister.

You are solely responsible for your own personal care, those core parts of your person that are classified physical, mental, emotional and spiritual. You cannot do this without a planned approach, without personal sharing with others or without maintaining a strong relationship with God. Do this well for the sake of the long, faithful journey that lies ahead.

Vision

The scripture states that "Where there is no vision…, the people perish;" (Proverbs 29:18) Someone has written the opposite truth, "with a vision the people flourish." Vision is the mental picture of a better tomorrow. This gives the energy we need to move toward the future. "As counselors, we should recognize that the Spirit of God is at work in people's lives long before they come for counseling, and that we attempt to silence the voice of the Spirit not recognizing there is hope by embracing it."[17]

Counselors have the unique privilege of creating a vision for themselves and also for the clients they see. "Tomorrow" thinking is a powerful force in people's lives. While we cannot create a tomorrow for

---

[17] John Pugh, "Improving Relationships through Spiritual Formation," *Marriage and Family: A Christian Journal*, Vol. 6, Issue 1, (2003): 90.

our clients, we can help them do so. Often this is the major force that keeps them moving forward. In the stage play "Annie," the red haired little girl steps to the front edge of the stage and boldly sings her song. "Tomorrow, tomorrow, I love you, tomorrow, you're only a day away!" We act out those words as we meet with clients. "As people act, they manifest their vision of marriage, the core vision of the marriage as it is perceived to actually be."[18] "People's marriages follow their vision. To affect the vision you systematically help refocus their view on faith acting through love."[19]

---

[18] Everett L. Worthington, Jr. and Douglas McMurry, *Marriage Conflicts* (Grand Rapids, Baker Books, 1997), 94.

[19] Everett L. Worthington, Jr. and Douglas McMurry, 94.

Chapter 3

Personal Spiritual Formation

**"Unless a living organism changes, it necessarily dies.
The one thing that does not change is a
fossil – and a fossil has been dead for a very long time."
(William Barclay)**

The apostle Paul prayed that, while he engaged in sacrificial service to God, he would not lose his focus and become a discarded, useless tool for God's service. (1 Corinthians 9:27) Counselors who are engaged in the spiritual service of helping others must always attend to spiritual formation and enrichment in their own lives. Here are the key elements of a counselor's spiritual formation regimen.

Prayer

Because prayer is a moment-by-moment, hour-by-hour practice in Christian Counseling, it comes first in this section. The scriptures tell us to "pray without ceasing", or "pray continually." (1 Thessalonians 5:17) Daily prayer is for insight, discernment and guidance. It is also for clear thinking, confidence and peace in the many moments of stress.

The question is not, "do we pray with our clients?", but "what form of prayer do we use?" Sometimes prayer is oral to open, close or use in a counseling session. More often it is silent. Awareness always changes things in a counseling session and in prayer. Each session, and each new awareness, will dictate your direction in prayer. Ministers should also be alert to know the times not to pray. The routine of using prayer to begin or end a session may need to be changed. When clients ask for prayer, counselors need to be conscious of why the request. We should discover the cause for the prayer request and if it needs to be fully discussed first. Perhaps the reason for the request is to deflect or detour the discussion from the core issue.

Bible Study and Meditation

The purpose of this discussion is not to give you a theological lesson about the Bible or the work of the Holy Spirit, but to guide you to use what you believe in your personal life and practice. The Bible is a central textbook and a resource book in Christian counseling. We are to use it regularly, accurately, creatively, gently and prayerfully.

However, in your personal spiritual formation the Scriptures have a more important place. Often our personal familiarity with the Bible keeps us from gaining the daily insights that God has stored there for our benefit. I have found the practice of daily scripture reading, accompanied by a companion devotional book, to be an enriching practice.

My personal Bible study for a weekly teaching or learning class experience has been a constant means of spiritual formation. Another meaningful source of spiritual enrichment for me has been the practice of always being engaged in reading a devotional book. By this I mean books read for devotional purposes, not books planned for daily devotions. I also use them in daily devotional times.

Corporate Worship

Corporate worship is our public response to the grace and goodness of God. It is our expression of His "worth-ship" in our lives. We worship best when this is a time of giving ourselves more fully to God and presenting ourselves to Him for His pleasure. Public worship services encourage us to connect with others who are followers of Jesus. This reminds us that our spiritual journey is not a "solo" walk, but is most effective when we join others in the journey. In worship we relate to God by relating with fellow Christians.

Group Experiences

The promise of the scripture is that "where two or three are gathered together in My name, I am there in the midst of them.". (Matthew 18:20) Small group experiences have been a major spiritual formation tool for churches and other Christian movements. I have found

35

that either meeting with a formally structured small group or gathering informally with a cluster of friends always enriches my life spiritually. The key ingredient in these experiences has been the dialogue, the give and take of sharing with others that is for me both a place of receiving and giving.

Service Opportunities

It is very easy to complete each day's work and each week's schedule of seeing clients and feel we have done our service for God and mankind. However, for our own personal spiritual enrichment, we gain by regularly engaging in some Christian service apart from our vocation. Whether it is serving food at a rescue mission, visiting a senior adult facility, meeting with a children's group or engaging in a mission trip, we will find fresh experiences of spiritual enrichment that rewards us personally.

Gaining Your Footing and Your Voice

To conclude this chapter about preparation, consider your personal challenge to "gain your footing" and "find your voice". As I have worked with beginners in this field, whether students in internship or new counselors with proper credentials, I have observed that they struggle to "get their footing" and "find their voice". Let me explain those terms.

The first challenge is to get your footing or "sea legs" as a competent and confident counselor. This is the process of integrating your sense of calling, personal values, educational preparation and life experience into a solid foundation from which to counsel. You gain this through counseling experience, coaching, contemplation and the guidance of the Holy Spirit. You want to feel that you are on a solid footing when you meet your clients.

The second challenge is to find your voice, your ability to know what to say and when and how to phrase your counsel in a competent and confident manner. When counselors respond to clients or the public, they need a sense that they speak healing and helpful words. In the best of times, one's voice conveys the tone and message that God gives.

This is an opportunity to address one critical area for ministers, voice and speech patterns. Like any professional role, the minister's role of preaching, teaching and "church-talk", will influence voice and speech patterns. It is very important for the counseling minister to develop a conversational style of talking that is warm and inviting, but not artificially "ministerial". The ability to listen intensely and respond in quiet, "real life" ways is essential.

Getting your footing and finding your voice signifies that you are maturing in the ministry of counseling.

Chapter 4

Getting Started

**"Nothing in your life is so insignificant, so small,
that God cannot be found at its center."
(Sister Frances Dominica)**

Having established an understanding of the personal characteristics of the Christian counselor, we need to explore how you do the work of the Christian counselor, and more precisely, the minister-counselor. We will discuss how you proceed as a counselor. In the remaining sections, you will notice that I am presenting the materials with the pronoun "we." This is done because I practice counseling with a peer group. My official position is Director of Counseling at Master Resources Counseling Center. I also maintain a full schedule of clients, which keeps me fulfilled in my ministry and current in my understanding of counseling. We have several other counselors who practice in our counseling center.

Choosing the Setting

After dealing with those issues of qualifying as a counselor, the first step is choosing a favorable setting for your counseling practice. Your personal status as a minister may dictate some parts of this while economic issues may dictate others. If you are a full time minister of a specific church where you have an office, your choice may be to conduct your counseling sessions there. Questions you will need to consider are these:

1. Is this an attractive, pleasant setting in which to bring a client?

2. Is there a way to provide privacy to your clients as they come in, wait for the appointment time and leave?

3. Is there adequate space for seating of two or more persons?

4. Are there adequate restroom facilities available?

5. Will your clients feel free to come into the church building or will this limit your practice?

6. Is the exterior area safe at night?

7. What will be the arrangements you make with the church if this will be your private practice and what will be the attitude of the church members who, coming and going at the church, will see this happening?

8. Will the church be liable in any legal issues?

This list only begins the questions you will need to consider. On the other hand, you may be a minister who is bi-vocational, expecting to be a full-time counselor and desiring to conduct your counseling ministry off-site from the church. You may need to consider these questions.

1.   What will be the arrangements, space and finances that you will make to have your practice?

2.   Can you afford these arrangements, both personally and professionally?

3.   Is there adequate security, privacy, staff, space, parking and other physical concerns for both your clients and yourself?

4.   Is this an attractive, welcoming place where clients can be relaxed?

5.   Some of the questions in the previous paragraph will also apply here.

There will be other concerns to address if you choose this setting for your counseling ministry.

Your choice about the room where you meet clients is very important. You will notice that each client's first actions will be to survey your meeting room. They are looking for clues that will help them be comfortable or cause them to be on guard. A warm, comforting room is the first requirement. The presence of bookshelves and diplomas may help them know you are professionally qualified. However, the presence of soft furniture in warm colors will help them to be comfortable emotionally.

How you choose to present yourself is a personal matter, but it has professional significance. Some counselors choose to dress very formally in business suits while others may choose to wear the jeans and golf shirts of recreational dress. The best approach is to be someplace in the center of these two extremes.

While each person has developed his/her own style of greeting people, as a counselor, your greeting must be both comforting and confident. Because you will be greeting people who are bringing problems to you, it is wise to temper your personal approach to understanding where your clients are. As in dress style, your speech style needs to be clearly thought out. This is the place for the "preacher" role to be laid aside and your warm, conversational style to be used. The axiom is "you only have one time to make a first impression." Truthfully, you only have a few minutes with each client to establish a good impression.

If the persons are members of your congregation or known to you in some other way, you may not have to spend much time introducing yourself and your experience in counseling. If not, you will want to develop a brief statement introducing yourself and your counseling ministry. At this point remember that you are in the three roles of minister, teacher and counselor, and you may want them to see you primarily as one of these. Help them feel comfortable because they will likely be nervous, scared and restricted in what they say. You will want to arrange the seating so they can see each other and be close. These preliminary things give you opportunity to note body language and attitudes.

Initial Interview

The initial session is used primarily to gather understanding about the couple and their issues. However, this process must have places where a positive voice is heard and hope is encouraged. If the session is dominated by the criticisms and complaints of each person, one of the persons may not return for the following sessions.

The persons may have some initial questions to ask about you as a minister or as a counselor. You will want to stress confidentiality and ask each person to sign a statement of confidentiality. You may want to sign one with them. Point out that this agreement covers not only what they tell you but also what you tell them. Your reputation can be damaged by being misquoted or quoted out of context by a client. This and other guidelines reviewed in the initial session will be more fully addressed in the later section on ethics. You will want to assure the clients that they are in a safe place and that everything will remain confidential unless there is a threat of harm to themselves or others, child neglect or child abuse is evident, or a judge should order that confidentiality be broken.

At this point you ask the persons to explain their reasons for coming to this session. The best way I have found to do this is to ask one person to go first and other person to listen. Each will be given equal opportunity to state their case. At this point you clearly ask each of them not to interrupt or comment on what is being said.

As this dialogue is happening, the counselor must listen very closely with specific questions in mind.

1. What are the problems and how does each person interpret them?

2. What efforts have been made for change and why have they not worked?

3. How are the problems affecting each of them personally and how are they reacting to the problems?

4. Are there specific "broken areas" for each person such as depression, anxiety, alcohol and drug use, levels of dysfunction, personality disorders, or ability to have insight?

5. What do they each desire to accomplish through the counseling process?

6. What are their expectations of you as their counselor?

Your responsibility during this process is to be a careful listener and note taker and to ask for clarification for the statements that you do not understand. Your goal during this time is to gain a good understanding of their relationship issues.

After this time of expression, you will be ready to ask exploratory questions. You may want to ask questions such as these:

1. What does each of you see as a healthy marriage?

2. What changes will you need to make to accomplish that?

3. What are the areas where you need learning and coaching?

4. What are the areas where you need to stop actions and attitudes?

5. What are the areas where you need to start actions and attitudes?

6. How committed is each of you to your marriage?

7. Are there any third parties influencing the marriage?

8. How willing is each of you to be accountable and responsible for improvement in the marriage?

45

This process gives you a good sense of how open and willing each of them is to work on their relationship.

At this point, you as the counselor will make some significant decisions. While you may not yet have enough understanding to make a good decision, your ability to move forward with the couple will hinge on decisions you make early in the counseling process.

1. Would you accomplish anything significant by seeing them the next time as a couple?

2. Or would you serve them best by scheduling individual sessions with each person? One or both persons usually will have personal issues that directly influence the marriage. Sometimes the marriage is so emotionally charged that each spouse needs to learn various skills to help improve the relationship. This may require individual counseling before you can focus on the relationship.

3. Should you refer this couple to another counselor?

Let us explore the issue of referral thoroughly before moving forward in the counseling process.

To Refer or Not Refer

This is an ever-present issue for all counselors, not just ministers. Every counselor finds himself facing clients that present to him/her possible personal issues. Some of the questions to consider are:

1. Are the needs presented beyond the training and experience of the counselor?

2. Is there an obvious dual relationship that will hurt the counselor's ability to help them? (Dual relationships are discussed later in this book). This can include counseling a family member or personal friend. Has the counselor had an experience with this person that would make counseling difficult?

3. What are the time constraints in assuming the responsibility of being their counselor? Can you give this couple adequate time and attention?

4. Are you choosing to do this to meet your own personal needs, when you should refer?

5. Are there personal issues of the counselor that would affect the counseling relationship negatively?

6. Are they seeing another counselor for the same issue?

7. Is this a good fit for you and, what are the things that may affect your effectiveness as a counselor?

These and many more questions can be considered as you choose to proceed. The minister-counselor has specific areas to consider before proceeding.

1. What is your present relationship with one or both of these persons that could affect your effectiveness negatively? Do these persons have any power over the minister in the framework of the church? Are there experiences in the past that could hurt the counseling process?

2. What are the many dual relationships that are shared by minister and clients? How will these be handled during times of stress and confrontation by each party?

3. What are the time constraints this responsibility brings? Is the minister opening himself or herself to greater responsibilities?

4. In what way would you be seen as a competitor to other members of the congregation, such as a professional counselor?

5. Can the minister's best role for this couple be that of minister-supporter? Would the minister's role be threatened by being the counselor and damage relationships to the church-at-large?

We assume in these questions that for most ministers the role of minister is a primary role and that being a counselor is secondary.

As a professional therapist and a minister's wife, I advise ministers to refer whenever possible. Often the initial interview session is all that is needed to motivate a minister to refer. There are many negative ramifications to being the counselor to members of your church. Members often leave a church after confessing their deepest sins to the minister. Many people leave a minister's office quoting the minister on some issue that negatively reflects on the minister. The minister's time is usually scarce, even in a sixty- hour workweek. The people most affected by a busy minister are often his family. In the Christian Standard magazine, Phil LeMaster spoke of the high cost of marital counseling by stating there can be a terrible price to pay in marital counseling – for the counseling preacher! He mentions the cost of time, minister-member relationship danger, possibly his position and his family.[20]

There are many available Christian counselors. Other ministers in the area can identify these for you. You will spend your valuable time wisely by getting to know the Christian counselors in your area. They will

---

[20] Phil LeMaster, "The High Cost of Marital Counselors," *Christian Standard Publishing Co.*, Cincinnati, December 2006, 33.

be glad to discuss with you their beliefs, approach, financial policies, and local references that affirm their effectiveness.

Goal Setting and Action Planning

Establishing goals is very important in building a plan of treatment. The questions asked in the initial interview and their answer shape this plan. These questions are designed to define what the client couple wants to accomplish and how they see themselves participating. As the counseling minister makes notes of these answers, the key issues emerge.

Using these issues as the basis for planning, goals are established that address each specific issue. These goals are clearly stated in the counselor's notes. When practical, the counselor should interpret these goals to the client couple and get their input. The client may have participated in the establishment of these goals. Often goals establishment would not be wise in the early sessions, but can be used later as guiding factors in the treatment.

A plan of treatment is constructed by the counselor for each key issue. This becomes a roadmap to change. Accomplishment of small steps gives confidence for larger goals.[21] A good plan of treatment will produce two basic types of change, external change in behavior and internal change in attitudes and viewpoints. The effective counselor will recognize such changes and affirm the client for their progress.

There are three categories of clients, according to Gary Oliver: visitors, complainants and customers. Each of these has a different motivation for coming to counseling.

1. The **visitor** comes for help because someone else wants them to come;

2. The **complainant** comes because the behaviors of other people are causing them problems, and

3. The **customers** come because they are willing to resolve the issues.[22]

An understanding of these categories will help in establishing your goals and action plans for clients.

---

[21] Timothy Clinton and George Ohlschlager, *Competent Christian Counseling* (Colorado Springs: Waterbrook Press, 2002), 236-237.

[22] Gary J. Oliver, Monte Hasz and Matthew Richburg, *Promoting Change Through Brief Therapy in Christian Counseling* (Wheaton: Tyndale House Publishers, Inc., 1997), 139.

Establishing Clear Boundaries and Rules

As discussed in previous sections, the counselor must operate within widely accepted boundaries and internal space we call "comfort zone." Dr. Henry Cloud states, "When we think of boundaries, we think of limits. Boundaries give us a sense of what is a part of us, and what is not a part of us."[23] Boundaries are mental lines we draw to protect ourselves and limit our responsibilities. When these lines are crossed we are able to sense the warning signs of discomfort, anxiety or fear. Some of these lines involve moral issues, some ethical issues and some involve emotional and mental sensitivities.

There is not a comprehensive list of all rules and boundaries for the counselor-minister. However, the following questions can aid the discovery of boundary issues.

1. What are the harmful elements in this issue? Usually we can define the positive or helpful elements more easily. There is always a negative side to boundary issues and we must clearly define those also.

---

[23] Henry Cloud, *Changes that Heal* (Grand Rapids: Zondervan Publishing House, 1992), 92.

2. What damage could be done? For instance, a confidence broken

    or personal opinion spoken may seem harmless at first, but can do

    harm to others, to self and to careers.

3. What protective boundaries should I learn and commit myself to?

    These come from personal experiences or observation of others.

However you learn them, make note of these for future reference.

Cloud and Townsend maintain that developing clear Biblical boundaries

can improve relationships and emotional well-being. "Controlling their

own thoughts, attitudes, feelings, choices and actions, and accepting

responsibility for their effects on relationships are some of the most

important tasks for which people are responsible. The Bible gives the

parameters or boundaries necessary to accomplish these tasks, but past

experiences of painful relationships will often distort these biblical

principles, causing them to be ignored or misapplied."[24]

Establishing a Healthy Relationship

In recent medical news, a new surgical procedure was described as

much more accurate, effective and safe than standard procedures. It

described how a trained surgeon could be more effective by using a robot

---

[24] Jerry White and Hayden D. Center, Jr., "Influencing Change in Bowenian Differentiation of Self Through Cloud and Townsend's Boundaries Instruction," (*Marriage and Family; A Christian Journal,* Vol 5, Issue 4, 2002), 527.

to do the surgery. The robot was more precise than human hands, the view of the surgical space greatly enlarged from a camera put very close to the wound and the recovery time was shortened because there was no bruising as when done with human hands.

In contrast to that procedure, counseling is a face-to-face encounter with human beings. That encompasses the differing emotions, rational thinking and verbal expression of these persons in the counseling setting. What we have described here is called relationships, or the process of relating. The first and most important task of a counselor is to build a positive, workable relationship with clients.

As you begin the counseling sessions following the initial interview, individually or as a couple, you are exploring how relationships are working in the life of your clients. For instance, you should inquire about the person's support system. This is very important to the couples that have serious troubles. Encourage them to enlist supporting persons who do not give them advice or tell them what to do, but do give active listening and offer to pray with and for them. Also engage the persons in what they expect to receive from the counselor. Stress that in the counselor relationship there must be accountability, responsibility and a commitment to the process. Tell them that we are not in the business of fixing problems, but we are in the business of viewing the problem "with a new set of eyes." While many come to counseling to get the other person "fixed", counselors position themselves as objective listeners who are experienced in handling conflicts and motivating them to make change. You should see clients as whole persons composed of five core areas: mental, physical, emotional, social and spiritual. If any one of those areas is out of balance or wounded, the relationship will not function properly.

Once you have listened and built rapport to address the couple, begin to define the problems as you hear them. First, explain the counseling process as a way of approaching their problems. Insist that this is a joint effort with the three of you working as a team to discuss how change can happen. Counselors often discuss the issues by displaying marriage as a wheel that must move forward in order to grow. The spokes of the wheel represent the problems or issues presented by the parties. The task is to repair the wheel and get it moving forward. This will involve things to be learned, negative attitudes and actions to be replaced, and new commitments to be made.

At the close of the first initial session counselors like to give homework. Sometimes there are obstacles to doing that, but the homework does help in focusing on a direction. There are many possibilities for homework after that first session. You may use a couple inventory, asking them to write a brief history of their marriage, or you may address questions such as what is positive about your relationship? What do you want in your marriage and how are you going to accomplish what you want? Ask the couple to work on these questions together or separately depending on issues or conflicts. You may also ask them to address what a healthy marriage looks like or what are the traits of a healthy marriage. This clarifies their perspectives, which can be discussed in the next session.

Let us address a very important issue in the first or early sessions. The counselor is responsible for assessing the possibility that one of the persons may be considering doing harm to themselves or others. If a suicidal tendency exists, establish a safety plan and contract with the parties on what needs to be done should that occur. Other areas of concern should be covered, such as medications, drug and alcohol use or health related problems.

The best length for a counseling session is a range of 50 minutes to one hour. Lengthy sessions can tire one of the persons and create despair or anxiety. Circumstances such as this are handled best in small, bite-size blocks of time.

The counselor is responsible for setting the pace and schedule for counseling process. Generally counseling sessions work best on a weekly schedule, usually the same day and hour each week. Definite appointments must be made and emphasized as part of the commitment each person makes to the process. A good schedule model is six to eight sessions for a couple with progress reviews held in session four and eight.

Session one: The initial interview includes a closing discussion on whether they feel comfortable with the counselor and want to come back.

Session two: Individual sessions for the two persons may be scheduled in the same week or on the same day.

Session three: The couple meets together with the counselor to review findings from the individual sessions and how they impact the marriage issues.

Session four: This will be a time of intensive discussion with the couple about the changes initiated during this period, the problems of the marriage and a review of progress in the counseling process

Session five: The counselor may review homework, discuss progress, and continue with interventions for healing and growth.

Session six: Another session of review provides time to repeat areas of change, to address old or new challenges, and to confront areas of challenge. At this time discuss with the couple what needs to be done next and how they feel about their progress.

Keep in mind that sessions often do not go this smoothly. This is a practical format for the minister-counselor. Future sessions should be scheduled as long as noticeable progress is being made. Significant progress seldom happens without the use of scheduled counseling sessions. Sessions may continue on a weekly basis according to the progress of the couple. Additional sessions may be structured every other week or third week to continue progress. This needs to be carefully discussed with the couple.

A Caution About Legal Matters

As minister-counselor it is important to be aware of and to maintain professional and legal standards. You can never be too cautious of situations that could have ramifications and ultimately negative results. In the intake process it is important that all of these matters be covered and that the counselor have an agreement with the client or clients to continue

58

with the counseling process. The following are simplified versions of the legal matters related to counseling couples. An excellent resource for legal matters in ethics is *Issues and Ethics in the Helping Professions;* Corey, Corey, and Callanan.[25]

Informed Consent

If the minister-counselors are concerned about legal matters, then they cannot take the rights of clients lightly. Informed consent means that the clients have the right to be informed of the purpose and nature of treatment, evaluation, educational and training procedures, and they have freedom of choice if a counselor is engaged in any type of research. Other content areas involved are: (a) what is involved in the counseling process, (b) a description of the therapist credentials and training, (c) fees or cost involved, (d) length and termination of therapy, (e) diagnostic information and (f) benefits and risk of treatment. Counselors need to inform the client of these questions: (a) what are the goals, (b) what services will be provided, (c) what is expected of the client, (d) what are the risks and benefits, (e) what are the qualifications of the counselor, (f) what is the fee

---

[25] Gerald Corey, Marianne Schneider Corey and Patrick Callanan, *Issues and Ethics in the Helping Professions* (Belmont: Brooks/Cole, 1993), 85-104.

structure, (g) how long will counseling last and (h) what exactly does confidentiality mean?[26]

Confidentiality

Often there are several terms used here, such as confidentiality, privileged communication and privacy. The three are related to each other. Counselors have an ethical and legal responsibility not to disclose any information except for specific reasons. There are limits to confidentiality. (Example, pg. 64) Those reasons are: harm to oneself, harm to someone else, circumstances of child abuse or child neglect, or if disclosure has been court ordered. When the client's condition indicates that there is clear and imminent danger to self or others, counselors have a duty to warn. Other professionals are helpful in giving guidance in this situation. If confidentiality is broken, it is important to inform the client and ask the client to participate in the process of reporting.[27]

Privileged communication is a legal term and means to protect the client in court situations. There are privileged-communication laws to ensure the client that personal and sensitive information will be protected.

---

[26], Gerald Corey, Marianne Schneider Corey and Patrick Callanan, *Issues and Ethics in the Helping Professions* (Belmont: Brooks/Cole, 1993), 86-88.

[27] Corey, Corey, Callanan, 102-104.

Privacy means that persons can choose their own circumstances and time to share or withhold their beliefs, behavior and opinions to others.[28]

Dual Relationships

According to the book *Issues and Ethics,* dual relationships are any situations when we blend a professional relationship with a client with whom we have another kind of relationship.

Some examples of these include: combining roles of teacher and counselor, providing counseling to a relative or friend's relative, socializing outside therapy sessions, becoming emotionally or sexually involved with a client or former client (ministers are especially vulnerable to this situation), and combining the role of supervisor and therapist.[29] As a minister-counselor, dual relationships can present complex situations. This is a reason I highly recommended that ministers refer. If the minister is trying to perform more than one role with clients there may be a boundary issue. In this case, is the minister-counselor trying to meet his or her own financial, social or emotional needs? Not all dual relationships are unethical, but in a counseling setting there might be legal or personal ramifications.

---

[28] Corey, Corey, Callanan, 103.
[29] Corey, Corey, Callanan, 95.

Referrals

In considering referrals, a basic question must be answered by the counselor. Can I work effectively with this couple? It is important to assess your own concerns honestly. Referrals can be appropriate when moral, religious, or political values are involved in the client's situation, or when problems are presented. The counseling minister needs to know his own boundaries, professional training and personal issues when deciding whether or not to make a referral. Also it can be clearly understood that the minister is only into short-term counseling. Therefore, you need some idea of knowing when to refer and how to present this to the client openly.

Records and Progress Notes

Records and note taking are important in case of any questions, legal action or concerns. It is important to have in those records the intake information, your policies and procedures, financial agreements, signed copies of confidentiality and client rights, plan of treatment, goals, diagnostic data and possible interventions. Keep your files locked in a file cabinet or desk. At each session memory notes are helpful. (example, pg. 65) These are really for the counselor to be aware of what is going on and what has been covered in each session. Actually, a progress note is called a "memory note." (Exp. pg 65) Without some help it is difficult to remember what has been the focus, direction for the next session and a measurement of progress.

Financial Issues/ Fees

Clients have a right (client rights) to reasonable financial arrangements. Collecting a fee is a delicate matter. It is helpful if you have an established guideline for fees. Often people want to file their insurance and the counseling minister may or may not be a provider. We have discovered that charging a fee is important. Clients work harder and listen better if they know there is a cost. They feel more accountability and responsibility to the process. Also it helps with relationships, and it becomes compensation for the counselor's time and efforts. This information needs to be covered in the beginning. To be fair, the counseling minister may want to have a sliding-scale fee determined by the amount of the client's income and the number of dependents. In our office we begin this process when the client completes the initial intake form prior to the first session. In that form the clients may state their income, asking for a reduced fee. This information is one of the first things discussed in the first session, and a negotiated fee is established.

Statement Of Confidentiality

It is our policy that a basic right of every client is the right to confidentiality. Confidentiality is both an ethic principal and a law which prevents disclosures about clients and their care without their expressed **written** permission, except in medical emergencies, cases of child abuse, threat to the lives of self or others, or by Court Order.

If you have further questions about confidentiality, please feel free to discuss this with your therapist.

_____   _____

Client Signature   Date

*Adapted from various sources

Suggested Sample Form
Memory Note

Service Date_____ **Client Name**_____

Session Content (Focus, Interventions, Activities)

_____
_____
_____
_____
_____
_____
_____

Mood: Appropriate, Depressed; Angry; Anxious; _____

Thought Processes: Goal directed; Disorganized; Alert; _____

Suicidal Potential _____

Safety Plan Discussed

_____
_____

Goals Addressed

_____
_____
_____

Progress Toward Goals: Slight Progress   Fair Progress   Substantial Progress No Progress

Date/Focus of next session (homework, etc.)

_____
_____

Counselor Signature and date:

_____

*Adapted from various sources

Chapter 5

Tools in the Process of Christian Counseling

**"People do not enter our lives to be coerced or manipulated, but to
enrich us by their differences
and to be graciously received in the name of Jesus."
(Elizabeth Canham)**

The minister-counselor needs to be informed and experienced with

various procedures and options available and useful during the counseling

process. As you proceed in the sessions of your plan of treatment, you

may want to review one or all of the tools described in this section. You

will find in this section explanations and experience in using these tools to

make our work more effective.

Making the Assessment

Because an accurate assessment is so important to the counseling

process, there are a number of approaches that must be considered. The

intake session is very important to the assessment because there you

identify the areas of information needed and the questions that can be used

to obtain that information.

1. What is their reason for seeking counseling at this time?

2. How long have they experienced these problems or conflicts?

3. What precipitated their coming to counseling? Was it an event or circumstances that made them realize they needed help?

4. What has been tried or done to help with the problem?

5. How do they state the problem? (physical problems, medication, drug and alcohol use, personal problems, depression, anxiety, grief, etc.)

6. Describe their family of origin.

7. Describe their past marriages, children, length of marriage, support systems, suicidal tendencies, etc.

8. What would they like to accomplish in coming for counseling, and what expectations do they have of the counselor?

9. What needs to happen for things to be better?

With this information, plus observation of the non-verbal and verbal communication styles of each, the counselor begins an assessment based on his training and experience. After years of counseling, a counselor develops a sixth sense for this occasion.

As stated earlier, all of us are composed of five core areas: mental, physical, emotional, social and spiritual. Whenever one of these areas is out of balance or wounded, all of them are impacted. A possible illustration to explain this is of an automobile with five pistons. When one of those pistons is not functioning properly, all of them are affected and the car does not perform well. In a marriage relationship when one of the areas does not function well, the marriage gets out of balance and does not function properly. We provide dry erase boards in each office to illustrate this to clients and list the problems we have heard as causing things to be out of balance.

Once these questions have been discussed, a preliminary assessment can be made. Then a counseling plan is built for continuing work or other recommendations. Typically each client is asked if he/she feels comfortable with the counselor, and the counselor makes an assessment of his/her comfort in continuing counseling. While in the vast majority of times the process continues, the client has the option of not continuing and the counselor has the option of referral.

Case Formation and Plan of Treatment

After the initial interview and assessment, such important questions as "Can this marriage survive?" and, "What must be done to save it?" are considered. This may take a second session where the attitudes of the individuals are tested to discern the best possibilities.

Individual sessions are very valuable in continued assessment and in constructing a Plan of Treatment. One should always assume there are two sides to every story. Each couple is unique and their uniqueness

must be recognized and appreciated without bias.

The Case Formation is tailored to fit the problems and struggles of

each couple. Counselors learn and develop explanations for the causes

and influences of human behavior to guide their thinking. The ability to

clearly define issues and direct the process is case formation. Christian

counselors need a Biblical understanding of people's problems to achieve

God honoring solutions.[30] The Plan of Treatment (example pg. 70&71) must

include goals that are realistic and attainable. Couples who feel some

improvement toward a realistic goal will find encouragement to work

harder. The Plan of Treatment will also include homework, a way for the

couple to express commitment to the process. At no time should the

counselor be the one who is working the hardest on the marriage.

Individual Counseling

Sessions with the individuals in the marriage are very necessary to

the success ofthe counseling experience. Often one member of the

marriage intimidates the other partner and that person is unable to speak

freely in the joint session.

---

[30] Timothy Clinton and George Ohlaschlager, *Competent Christian Counseling* (Colorado Springs: WaterBrook Press, 2002), 69-70.

Suggested Sample Form
Treatment Plan Initial Assessment For Ministers

Client _____ Date _____

Age_____ Phone (_____)_____-_____ Counselor_____

Referral Source _____

Presenting Problems/Precipitating Events

_____
_____
_____

Support Systems:_____

Medical Problems: _____

Family History: _____

Counselor's Observations

_____
_____
_____
_____
_____
_____
_____

Treatment/Recovery Goals

Issues	Goals	Objectives

1. _____

2. _____

3. _____

4. _____

Recommendations/ Immediate Action Taken:

_____
_____
_____
_____
_____
_____
_____
_____
_____
_____
_____
_____
_____

*Adapted from various sources

Sometimes one partner in the marriage has serious issues that must be worked on before the marriage can move forward, such as childhood trauma, wounds from a previous marriage, depression, anxiety disorders, personality disorders, such as borderline personality disorder, antisocial personality disorder and dependent personality disorders, to name a few.

Early in the counseling process the counseling minister is assessing the level of love and commitment each partner has for their spouse. "Most problems in marriage arise when partners do not value each other or actively devalue each other…if the root of marital problems is insufficient valuing or too much devaluing, the solution to them then, is to help partners attribute and show more value to each other and feel more love."[31]

In Harley's book *Fall In Love Stay In Love*, he discovered that "one of the most important reasons that couples were communicating so poorly, resolving their conflicts so ineffectively, and fighting so much was that they had lost their feeling of love. If your marriage was in trouble and I asked you what would it take for you and your spouse to be happily married again, what would you say? Again and again many couples have

---

[31] Everett L. Worthington, Jr. and Douglas McMurry, *Marriage Conflicts* (Grand Rapids: Baker Books, 1997), 40-41.

told me: 'We would be happily married again if we were in love.'"[32] "I began to encourage couples to try to do whatever it took to make each other happy and avoid doing what made each other unhappy. I simply asked each of them what the other could do that would make them the happiest, and whatever it was, that was their first assignment."[33]

The counselor needs to explore the persons' personal view of themselves, their view of their family of origin, and personality traits that create problems for them. Usually the counselor will explore with each person what is wrong in the relationship, how it is impacting him or her personally and what changes can be made to help the relationship.

The goal of the counselor in individual sessions is to help each partner improve the ability to function in the relationship and understand the problems of the other person. Often one of the marriage partners will see the need for long-term treatment in order to function better both in the marriage and in life at large.

---

[32] Willard F. Harley, Jr., *Fall In Love Stay In Love* (Grand Rapids: Fleming H. Revell, 2001), 12.

[33] Harley, 13.

Interventions

Interventions are the specific intentional actions a counselor asks a couple to perform to help repair the marriage. Interventions can be as simple as asking the couple to sit close together or as specific as giving a homework assignment of giving each other affectionate hugs each day. Interventions are determined by what the couple wants to accomplish, not just what the counselor wants to achieve. Consideration of key symptoms in the emotional, cognitive, behavioral, social and spiritual areas will help determine the types of interventions used.

Before establishing the interventions, the counselor must define specific goals for the counseling process. Some of these goals may include improving listening skills, areas of personal change, improvements in coping skills for stress and disagreements, and improvement in assessing the strengths and weaknesses of their partner. Goals often mirror the statements made by the persons of what they would like to achieve in the counseling process.

Specific interventions are planned actions that address the needs that have been identified, with the goal of improving the relationship. In a simplified form here are some suggested interventions.

1. Assign homework that involves the couple doing things together.

2. Identify family stressors and ways to reduce stress.

3. Suggest ways to change behaviors that impact positive changes in the relationship.

4. Teach problem-solving techniques.

5. Suggest individual therapy to address specific personal issues that are influencing the relationship.

6. Determine and establish healthy boundaries.

7. Practice specific communication skills and tools.

8. Have romantic experiences that are fun and relaxing.

9. Make a choice to forgive.

10. Suggest Family or group counseling for healing and growth.

The counselor will also consider interventions when a triangle has been built that is affecting the marriage relationship. Often one member of the marriage is over or under functioning and causing additional stress. Frequently there are issues dealing with blended families that cause conflict and misunderstanding. In such cases there may be need for family group sessions and/or individual counseling for other members of the family. "The main point of ministerial counseling is to help people solve their marital difficulties within a Christian context. It helps them understand problems within the context of their Christian life and apply the principle of faith through love to solve the problem."[34]

In my years of practice I have learned that married couples often suffer from a loss of love or not being in love. Their schedules, family responsibilities and outside interests rob them of any meaningful shared experiences. They need help in restoring their love.

Initially, I want them to tell me about how they met and fell in love. I want to know about what they did together, how they treated each other and pleasurable experiences they shared. Often I ask them when they noticed that this was missing in their lives. What were some of the identifiable experiences or causes that caused them to lose their love?

I have found two things that are effective in addressing this need. One, to give them a homework assignment to "do whatever it takes to make the other person happy." Have them ask what it takes to make the other happy. A second assignment is to have a "date night" the

---

[34] Everett L. Worthington, Jr. and Douglas McMurry, *Marriage Conflicts* (Grand Rapids: Baker Books, 1997), 140.

76

next week and every week during the counseling process. Coach them on how to make this a special night.

Spiritual Direction

Christian counselors believe that the core area of spirituality with couples is extremely important. Some clients are not receptive to their spiritual connectedness, and that is to be respected and accepted. However, the hope always remains that the door of opportunity will be opened for further inquiry and direction. Many clients have some spiritual experiences in their background, but have not incorporated it into their present life and marriage. They do not realize God's design for marriage or the importance of spiritual connection and growth as a couple. Often when spiritual direction is presented there are feelings of guilt and unconfessed sin. There are many cases where one partner tries to control the other through spiritual manipulation. "In marriage we face the choice of using the power of intimate knowledge for good or evil: to stay when it would be easier to leave, to lose one's life for the sake of another, to choose the higher calling, to live as Christ, to serve as life-affirming opposites to draw one another toward the salvation of wholeness. It is this journey of faith and choice that keeps us from hurting one another more often than we do. As each partner makes this daily, sometimes difficult, choice for good, he or she becomes more whole, creating a marriage reflecting God's intention. It is a noble calling, one in which we find our life by losing it."[35]

The counseling minister is first of all responsible for presenting "live Christianity," modeling faith, love, forgiveness and grace. The counseling minister has the open opportunity to integrate core Christian principles into the marriage relationship. "Counseling Christian couples together has many advantages; partners share important values and beliefs. Both perspectives are available. Communication can be seen, not just talked about, and the tendency to form alliances is diminished."[36]

In my counseling sessions with couples seeking to rebuild their marriages, I inquire about their Christian commitment and their church participation. This is one of the freedoms I have as an independent counselor and an acknowledged Christian counselor. Often they tell me that their church participation is seldom to none. Early in the counseling process I urge them to go to church the next Sunday and I

---

[35] Ginny Bridges Ireland, "I Know Who She Is," *Christian Reflections, Center for Christian Ethics, Baylor University* (April, 2006): 71..

[36] Jay E. Adams, *The Christian Counselor's Manual*, (Grand Rapids: Baker Book House, 1973),

always ask them in the next session if they did indeed attend church. Many couples respond positively to the church attendance stating they enjoyed doing an activity together.

One of the interventions or homework assignments I give to many couples is to have a regular, preferably daily, time to read the Bible together and pray. While one of the obvious benefits from this is improved communication, it also challenges them to review their Christian heritage and experiences. This often becomes a place where conversation and emotional love are renewed.

There are many times in my practice that I work with a couple where one of them has a much stronger commitment and practice of their faith than the other one. In individual sessions I often coach the stronger Christian on how to relate positively to their spouse through prayer and church participation. Couples with a healthy church life have a big advantage in rebuilding their marriages.

The counseling minister can carefully apply Biblical messages into his counseling conversations. The counseling minister may be seen as the ideal person to receive confession and repentance and assure the client of God's forgiveness. While the counseling minister is not expected to give a Bible lesson or sermon, giving spiritual instruction and direction is expected.

Group Counseling

Often couples will be helped by becoming a part of a couples group after their couple counseling. There they have the opportunity to see that other couples have problems and difficulties. Ministers have a wonderful opportunity to start groups or direct couples to a class that deals with the building of strong marriages. Group therapy is a great tool and resource for marriage problems. It also helps in building support systems for a couple in crisis.

Supervision and Case Consultation

The counseling minister needs to take a lesson from the medical community about the importance of peer accountability and support. Counseling is a work, like medicine, that has dramatic effect on the community at large. The counseling minister should establish relationships with other counseling practitioners long before they are needed. When things are not going well with a couple and problems emerge that are not anticipated, the counselor needs someone to call on for help.

In our counseling center, we have a cluster of counselors who are always ready to hear the fellow counselor out and give helpful feedback. This can happen at any stage of the counseling process. Due to the ethical rules of confidentiality, this must be done discreetly and with someone who is both willing and qualified to offer help. Make sure this is a professional person in the field of counseling. It is also important at this point to remember and accept your own limitations. As a counseling minister, it is very vital to remember your role as minister as well as counselor in these circumstances. If there is the possibility of a crisis that would impact the church and influence you as minister, a qualified person should be brought into the picture to help all parties.

Networking and Referrals

Having a network of professional peers is important not only for consultation, but also for referrals. There are many areas of mental heath that are outside and beyond a counselor's area of expertise. Maintain a list of mental health professionals that have been investigated and have received positive evaluations from clients that have been referred to them. A good rule of thumb is this – when in doubt, refer. The minister will often see a couple one time to express his concern and determine the best fit for the couple. One great source for referrals is the American Association of Christian Counselors. When possible, ask for the opportunity to visit or discuss by phone a counselor's philosophy of counseling, belief system and areas of expertise. It is important that you understand, when referring, all information is confidential. Ask your client to sign a release of information before speaking freely about your client.

Chapter 6

Tools For Effectiveness

"By people we are broken, and by people we are put together again."
(John Drakeford)

Assessment Tools

There are several assessment tools to use in couple therapy.
Inventories that give a variety of thought questions are useful to assess
marital evaluations, personality and personal problems. Occasionally, I
use two tools suggested by Norman Wright in his book *Marriage
Counseling*.[37] One is the MAI (Marital Assessment Inventory). The
inventory contains 11 pages of questions that provide all kinds of
information to help identify potential areas of conflict. This information
includes areas of family structure and background, marriage preparation,
qualities of the person, requests and expectations each has for the other
partner. Important topics are finances, family issues, spiritual relationship
and decision-making. The last part of the test helps the counselor in
knowing a good place to begin with the couple.

---

[37] Norman H. Wright, *Marriage Counseling* (Ventura: Regal Books, 1995), 87-89.

Other important information that can be gathered involves goals for counseling, commitment to stay in the marriage and the level of each person's commitment. This inventory helps in the counselor's approach with the couple and provides an effective tool for growth. The inventory can be helpful to the couple also. It becomes a great tool for the couple to complete prior to the first counseling session. The MAI can be obtained through Christian Marriage Enrichment 17821 17th Street #190, Tustin, CA 92680.

Another assessment tool is The Taylor-Johnson Temperament Analysis (T-JTA). This supplies information about the personality of each spouse. Typically this tool is used after the first or second session. However, some counselors choose to use this in the beginning. The test requires about 45-50 minutes to complete. This analysis helps the counselor to focus immediately on specific differences between the two. It is a good way to make an analysis of the marriage. The T-JTA can be used with individuals, couples and families.[38]

With the T-JTA you must take a training course to administer and work with the test. Many one-day seminars are available. The T-JTA is also available for a self-study training course. Write to Christian Marriage

---

[38] Wright, 93-94

Enrichment, 17821 17th Street #190, Tustin, CA 92680. Homework also

is a good assessment tool, especially homework that is done together.

Some specific boundaries need to be stated because homework is not a

platform for more conflict, but an opportunity to communicate in a non-

threatening manner.

Diagnostic Help

The counseling minister may or may not be into diagnosis. When

you realize there are some other personal problems going on such as mood

changes, anxiety disorders, personality disorders, etc., this may be a good

time to refer the couple to a trusted Christian therapist, psychologist, or

psychiatrist. For help in this area there are many resources available for

further knowledge. The book of diagnostic labels is the DSM-IV, which is

used by all trained and licensed therapists. You may want training in how

to use this tool. Other helpful resources available are: *Marriage*

Counseling by H. Norman Wright (this is a practical guide for ministers

and counselors), and one of my favorites is *Diagnosis and Treatment*

Planning in Counseling by Linda Seligman. Another good resource is *The*

Couples Psychotherapy Treatment Planner by O'Leary, Heyman, and

Jongsma, Jr. Consulting with a licensed therapist is also a helpful

resource.

Linking with a Mental Health Professional

For minister-counselors it is important to build a resource list of Mental Health Professionals. There are web sites that offer information. Ask other respected ministers about trusted Christian Therapists, Psychologists and Psychiatrists. Investigate and set up appointments with Mental Health people to discover what their Christian orientation is and what values are important to them. How they view people and counseling will give some idea of your connection with them. The American Association of Christian Counselors can be contacted at (800) 5-COUNSEL. Another good resource is Focus on the Family in Colorado Springs, Colorado.

Knowledge and Experience

Your knowledge and experience will strengthen or hinder your effectiveness in counseling. If you are a counseling minister it is important to know yourself, your beliefs and values. Counseling knowledge is found through training, reading, seminars, workshops and continuing education. Experience will greatly enhance your authority and concept of people. Putting yourself in the stereotypical role of a minister will hinder the empathic bond between you and the client. Also the minister-counselors would not want to place themselves in a vulnerable situation with others. This is definitely a place of danger for the minister, the client and the congregation. The minister hopefully would not want to counsel above his training and ability.

The Intuitive Factor

As therapists we lean heavily on our intuitive feelings. In other words, we listen to our gut. At times there are no guidelines or ethical questions, but something inside tells us this is a place of concern or danger. Even seeking out the help of a trusted minister friend does not feel right. As Christians, we believe we must be in tune with that intuitiveness of God's presence in our lives. Sometimes we move forward too quickly without considering the consequences or ramifications. Tread softly and consider all sides before jumping into the ring.

Establishing Personal and Professional Boundaries

Boundaries for any minister are important. Early in the first session with the couple, it is important to establish healthy boundaries. Your personal boundaries include what you can or cannot do outside the time allotted to the couple. These personal boundaries involve your own beliefs, values, the needs of your family and the needs and demands of the congregation. Putting your priorities in order includes personal boundaries. Professional boundaries are knowing and admitting your limitations, time and ethical requirements. Unhealthy boundaries create

mistakes, judgments, domination and time frames that may not be

conducive to the counseling relationship.

Chapter 7

Bringing Closure to the Counseling Process

"Reinforce the lessons that the individuals have
learned throughout counseling that Christianity is faith
working through love. Marriage like Christianity,
is about valuing others, caring enough to
place other's needs above one's own."
(Everett L. Worthington, Jr. and Douglas McMurry)

The process of marriage counseling could be a never-ending task.

Any relationship has its high and low times. Every relationship has some

area that would benefit from counseling. However, it is only realistic to

reach a termination point. Often we review the progress of the sessions

and ask the clients if they are ready to end the formal counseling process.

Most have come to a place of new hopefulness and new habits that help

them move on. Some may want to come back in two weeks, three weeks

or a month to evaluate their progress. The most challenging person is the

one who doesn't want to end the process and would come back for months

or even years if allowed.

Progress Assessment

As you assess the progress of the clients and discuss with them a

point of closure, there are five areas you will want to consider.

(1)   Intimacy

One of the needs we bring to marriage is our desire to be closely connected with a significant other in every area of our lives. We call that intimacy. Intimacy may be experienced both in activity and a walk in the park.

In the helpful book, *Marriage Conflicts*, authors Worthington and McMurry speak of "closeness" as a better way to describe this characteristic.[39] They point out that closeness is a quality that houses either intimacy, distance or co-action. This recognizes that a couple needs intimacy, some places of personal distance and time to just do things together. Because marriage partners have a strong need for intimacy and often measure the quality of their marriage by intimacy, this is a key area of assessment.

(2)   Communication

In most marriages, this is an area of continuing challenge. Every communication has at least three aspects:

1.   What is said (content)

2.   How it was said (tone)

3.   How it was heard by the receiver

---

[39] Everett L. Worthington, Jr. and Douglas McMurry, *Marriage Conflicts* (Grand Rapids: Baker Books, 1997), 63.

We could add to that the dimension of non-verbal communication and have enough material to write a book. One facet in communication is the degree of power that people assume in their words. "The roots of many communication problems in marriage, whether they are seen as misunderstandings, poor communication styles or attempts to control the marriage, are pride and power...communication difficulties will not be resolved unless the root causes of pride and power are addressed."[40] A key way of evaluating communication is by considering how each partner values the other by their communication. Prosser and Qualls state, "You have to practice it every day. Couples have to work across the years in the light of the changing realities of who they are as individuals."[41] The counselor will ultimately judge the quality of the couple's communication by how honest and transparent they present themselves to each other. Gary Collins suggest 5 steps of effective listening:

1. Build a relationship

2. Explore the problem

3. Decide on a course of action

4. Establish schedules

_____

[40] Worthington, Jr. and McMurry, 113.
[41] Prosser and Qualls, 76.

5.   Encourage people to apply what they learn by launching out on their own.[42]

(3)   Conflict Management

While that is a term used in many parts of our society, it is a significant part of the marriage relationship. Often one of the two people is the manager of conflict, either by their silence, avoidance or power language. "In a society that puts increasing value on work and fulfillment of the individual, someone has noted that the dangerous dilemma is how to find "me" without giving up "us." After a few years many couples find themselves staring at virtual strangers when they are alone together."[43] One result you would like to see in your clients' relationship is managing conflict through mutual submission.

Sometimes we are able to remove the area of major conflict in a marriage relationship or we are able to help the partners devalue the cause of conflict instead of devaluing each other. This is a complex area but it can be addressed with the same tools we use to explore healing for other areas.

----

[42] Gary Collins, *How To Be A People Helper* (Wheaton, IL., Tyndale, 1976), 30.

[43] Prosser and Qualls, 75.

(4)   Mental Attitudes

Everyone has this personal area of thinking and imagining. Clients can major in "stinking thinking" or "healing thinking", and we must help them choose the right one. Significant mental attitudes to consider are assumptions, expectations and presumptions.

Assumptions are one part of the mental framework. Assumptions can destroy people and others around them. By judging from some act or statement, a person assumes a certain condition to be the reality. If a partner does not speak or reach out to the spouse, the spouse assumes that the partner is angry with them. Has the counseling experience helped in this area? "They have to understand that the person they married at twenty-five isn't the same anymore at forty-five. On the days when the romantic side of love and commitment doesn't seem to be as real, the fact that we once loved a person enough to marry them may serve as a beacon we follow out of the darkness."[44]

Expectations are similar to assumptions but are even more dangerous. What one partner expects of the other, but never speaks of, can cause enormous damage. Often negative expectations become self-fulfilling prophecies for what will happen later. Marriage is one area that

---

[44] Prosser and Qualls, 76.

is loaded with expectations by the spouses, the extended family and the community.

Perceptions also qualify as dangerous mental activity. Most people have enough negative thinking that, when turned loose to explode, will destroy marriages and family. A perception is a conclusion arrived at from limited evidence.

All of these factors are active in the self-talk persons engage in by themselves. Soon the assumptions, expectations or perceptions become a reality from which to function. Romans 12: 1-2 advises us to ".. not conform any longer to the pattern of this world, but be transformed by the renewing of your mind."

(5)   Commitment

A fifth area to assess is the commitment level you see in each of your clients. A very practical activity for you and your client couple is that of forming a contract or covenant between the two persons. You may want to explore the difference between a contract and a covenant. Generally a contract is an agreement between two parties who agree to do reciprocal things for each other. A covenant, the marriage covenant for example, is based more on the welfare of the other person than on the duties to be performed.

A goal of all marriage counseling is to increase the level of commitment each partner has for the other one. While marriage is seen as a "need-meeting relationship", the emphasis is not on having our personal needs met, but on having the privilege of meeting another person's needs. Marriage is a life-long covenant that benefits each of the marriage partners in ways that are most significant to them.

Disengagement

Having found a way to bring closure and acknowledged progress in the counseling relationship, the minister-counselor must find a way to rebuild the relationship of minister and member. For some couples, this will be very easy. They are pleased with the experience, but also pleased with a sense of normalcy. For others there will be some issues.

A prominent issue is that the couple sees you in an entirely different light than before. You have walked with them through a very personal, private chapter of their lives. They may have concerns about your knowing too much about them, and they may not want to have regular contact with you in the future. In client relationships for professional therapists the rule is that the counselor does not acknowledge or visit with a previous client unless the client initiates the contact. Therefore, the minister-counselor should have a specific discussion with the client couple about these matters as they do closure on the counseling process.

It is possible for a client relationship with the minister to become negative, or "sour" as they say in medicine. The counseling minister will be wise to discuss this with the couple by making an intentional appointment and discussing it thoroughly.

The goal of the counseling minister is to help people know Christ and to grow in their discipleship to Him. The counseling minister will want to discuss this goal with them and help them engage in achieving this. Having other couples within the church to help facilitate growth in discipleship would be helpful. When persons have been embarrassed by this occasion, help them to be surrounded by love. Assure the persons that you are very anxious to serve as their minister and want to remain in their friendship and fellowship.

Chapter 8

Meanwhile, Back at the Church...

**"There are five gospels of Jesus Christ –
Matthew, Mark, Luke, John and You, the Christian.
Many people will never read the first four."
(Gypsy Smith)**

We have prepared this material for the Minister-Counselor, fully

understanding that most of our readers will be a minister first and then a

counselor. That dual role can often get out of focus. To borrow a phrase,

"time and advice is our stock and trade" and counseling is time

consuming. Counseling is also mentally and spiritually draining. It will

be easy to "get the cart before the horse" and not "keep the main thing the

main thing."

It is our conviction that the church, meaning churches large and

small, is the central tool in kingdom building. We all have leadership

roles in our local church and value both the fellowship and ministry

opportunities they provide. Our minister is a very important person in our

lives and on occasions where we have had specific need of him, he has

been faithfully present.

Your place as minister is extremely important. While you may help several people through counseling each week, you will help ten times or more that number in your preaching, leading and minister roles. Because of your interest in marriage and healthy families in your church, we would like to explore ways to help marriages as you serve as minister.

Your Modeling Impact

Most ministers and counselors are married persons. You have found that marriage is not easy for anyone. There are opportunities where your marriage and your interpretation of it will be a teaching occasion.

1. Your **priorities** will reflect your view of your marriage. Your use of time will speak of your priorities. Taking time for your marriage and family will be a witness. Your description of your family life and your explanation of why you can or cannot attend a meeting or an event will tell of your marriage priority.

2. Your **conversation** will value or devalue your spouse and family. Informal conversation will be analyzed and quoted when you speak of your spouse or your children. References in sermons and public speaking occasions will reflect your values. How you refer to your spouse and family in sermons is always diagnosed.

3. Your **public behavior** with your spouse and family becomes a witness of your love and commitment to those special people. Your displays of pride, love and patience for these family members will demonstrate that you truly care. When you "honor" your spouse and your children, people will see your witness and want to follow your example.

4. Your **preaching and teaching opportunities** are public times when it is very important that you "honor" specifically your spouse and your children. In sermons on or about family or marriage, in illustrations where you tell of marriages and families, the message is sent about the value you place on your home life. Honoring your spouse also is a wonderful way to ward off the possibility of temptation presenting itself to you.

5. Your **leisure activities and hospitality** will be a witness. Every minister needs leisure time in his schedule and regular opportunities for recreation. While it is exciting to enjoy the company of others of your gender and enjoy participating in recreational activities, your family needs you first. How you demonstrate your love for your family during leisure and play time is a good witness of your values.

6. Your **routine as minister** can be a witness. Needless to say, there are countless opportunities each day to demonstrate a positive witness of your love and faithfulness to your family. In the routine of hospital visits, meetings and personal contacts with congregational members, your witness of the place of the family in your life is always significant.

7. Your **role as a resource person** will speak of your family commitments. As you grow in a counseling ministry and understand more fully the challenges each person faces, you will be enlisted to help other churches, groups and individuals with your ministry. Organizing marriage retreats has been an enjoyable experience for me and my husband. Being invited to speak at workshops and dinners have been rewarding. Being called on by fellow ministers and others for counsel or encouragement will affirm your calling to this ministry.

You Will Make a Difference!

In your calling you join many others who are "ministers of hope." This book is presented with the vision of recruiting you to battle for the building and preservation of healthy Christian marriages. Can you imagine how many different individuals will be impacted by the building and preserving of just one healthy Christian marriage? There is no way to accurately calculate that number, but it will be enormous!

Where will you find your place in the battle for healthy Christian Marriages?

1. You can work to make your marriage a witness of healthy Christian marriages.

2. You can determine what your plan will be to assist couples struggling with martial issues.

3. You can decide to assist conflicted marriages to the best of your ability and then refer them to a profession Christian counselor.

4. You may decide to pursue your study of becoming an effective minister-counselor. The resources noted in this book will be a good starting point. Whatever you decide to do to strengthen the families of your church and community, you will make a difference.

Grace is your currency, faith is your stability and love is your vocabulary. People will seek you out years later to tell you how you impacted their lives. Others will come to you for help without any effort on your part. Continue to be strong in your faith, warm in your love, and

generous with grace as you represent Jesus!

> **"God grant me the serenity to accept the**
> **things I cannot change and courage to**
> **change the things I can and the wisdom to**
> **know the difference."**
> **(The Serenity Prayer; 1941)**

BIBLIOGRAPHY

Abel, Robert. *The Relationship Toolbox*. Denver: Valentine Publishing House, 1998.

Adams, Jay E. *The Christian Counselor's Manual*. Grand Rapids: Baker Book House, 1973.

Benner, David G. *Care of Souls*. Grand Rapids: Baker Books, 2000.

Clineball, H.J., Jr., *Basic Types of Ministeral Care and Counseling Resources for the Ministry of Healing and Growth*. Nashville: Abingdon, 1984.

Clinton, Timothy, and George Ohlschlager. *Competent Christian Counseling*. Colorado Springs: WaterBrook Press, 2002.

Cloud, Henry. *Changes That Heal*. Grand Rapids: Zondervan Publishing House, 1992.

Collins, G.R. *How to Be a People Helper*. Wheaton: Tyndale, 1976.

Collins, G.R. *The Biblical Basis of Counseling for People Helpers*. Colorado Springs: NavPress, 1993.

Corey, Gerald, Marianne Schneider Corey and Patrick Callanan. *Issues and Ethics in the Helping Professions* (4th edition). Belmont: Brooks/Cole, 1993.

Crabb, Larry. *The Marriage Builder*. Grand Rapids: Zondervan Publishing House, 1992.

Goodwin, Hilda. Marriage Counseling and the Minister. *Journal of Religion and Health*. Vol. 3, Issue 2. (January 1964). 176-183.

Harley Jr., Willard F. *Fall In Love Stay In Love*. Grand Rapids: Fleming H. Revell, 2001.

Huggett, Joyce. *Listening to Others*. Downers Grove: InterVarsity Press, 1988.

Ireland, Ginny Bridges. *I Know Who She Is. Christian Reflection.* (April, 2006). Waco: Center for Christian Ethics. Baylor University. 68-72.

LaHaye, Tim, and Beverly LaHaye. *The Act of Marriage*. Grand Rapids: Zondervan, 1998.

LeMasters, Phil. *The High Cost of Marital Counseling*. Cincinnati: Christian Standard Publishing Co, 2006.

Merrill, Dean. *Clergy Couples in Crisis*. Waco: Word Books, 1985.

Miller, Kathy Collard, and D. Larry Miller. *What's in the Bible for Couples*. Lancaster: Starburst Publishers, 2000.

O'Leary, Daniel K., Richard E. Heyman and Arthur E. Jongsma, Jr. *The Couple's Psychotherapy Treatment Planner*. New York: John Wiley and Sons, Inc., 1998.

Oliver, Gary J., Monte Hasz, and Matthew Richburg. *Promoting Change Through Brief Therapy in Christian Counseling*. Wheaton: Tyndale House Publishers, Inc., 1997.

Peck, Scott M. *The Road Less Traveled*. New York: Touchstone Books, 1978.

Prosser, Bo, and Charles Qualls. *Marriage Ministry*. Macon: Smyth and Helwys Publishing, 2004.

Pugh, John. Improving Relationships through Spiritual Formation. *Marriage and Family A Christian Journal*. Vol. 6, Issue 1. Forest: 2003.

Rainey, Dennis, and Barbara Rainey. *Starting Your Marriage Right.* Nashville: Thomas Nelson, Inc., 2000.

Seligman, Linda. *Diagnosis and Treatment Planning in Counseling.* New York: Plenum Publishing Corporation, 1996.

Weinberg, George. *The Heart of Psychotherapy.* New York: St. Martin's Griffin, 1996.

Wheat, Ed, and Gloria Okes Perkins. *Secret Choices.* Grand Rapids: Zondervan Publishing House, 1988.

White, Jerry, and Hayden D. Center, Jr. Influencing Change in Bowenian Differentiation Of Self Through Cloud and Townsend's Boundaries Instruction. *Marriage and Family A Christian Journal.* Vol. 5, Issue 4. 2002. 525-535.

Worthington, Everett L. and Douglas McMurry. *Marriage Conflicts.* Grand Rapids: Baker Books, 1997.

Wright, Norman H. *Marriage Counseling.* Ventura: Regal Books, 1995.

CPSIA information can be obtained at www.ICGtesting.com
Printed in the USA
LVOW051620240712

291324LV00004B/8/P